Skylar's Wings
From Misfit to Perfect Fit

written by

Debbie R. Magee

Illustrated by

Jack Oniel

Copyright ©2024 by Debbie R Magee

All rights reserved.

No part of the this book may be reproduced or used in any manner without the written permission of the copyright owner, except for the use of brief quotations in a book review.

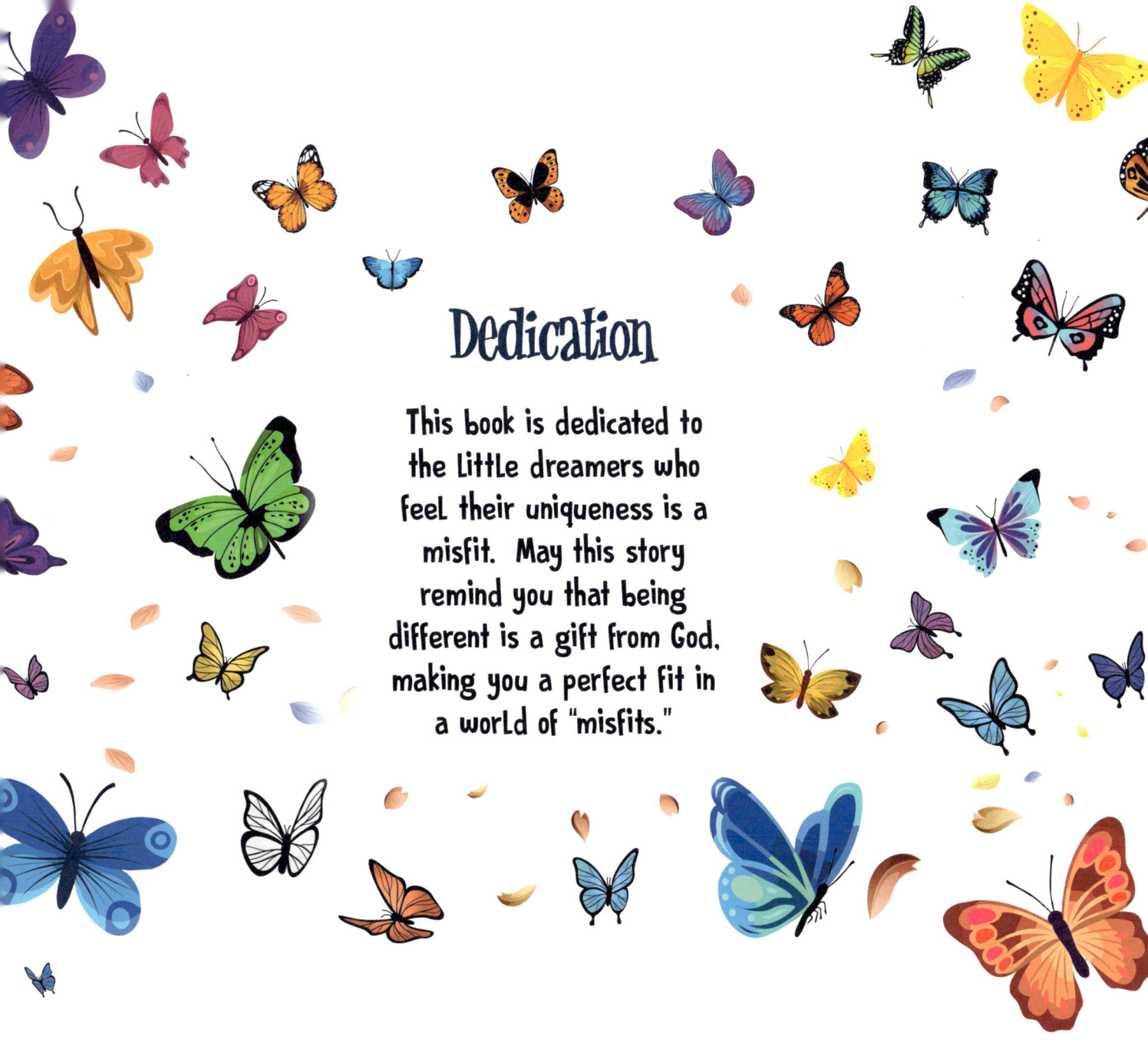

Dedication

This book is dedicated to the little dreamers who feel their uniqueness is a misfit. May this story remind you that being different is a gift from God, making you a perfect fit in a world of "misfits."

In the heart of Petal Falls was a meadow where dazzling butterflies fluttered.

Their beautiful wings covered the field with stunning colors, like a fallen radiant rainbow.

The butterflies floated through the air as if playing a dashing game of tag, chasing each other from flower to flower.

The entire meadow was their playground.

On a sweet-smelling daisy was a tiny butterfly named Skylar. In amazement, he watched the other butterflies, admiring their elegant wings.

Skylar compared his wings to the wings of other butterflies. He felt like a misfit, as his own had mismatched patterns.

Skylar hid between the soft petals of a daisy to avoid being seen.

Feeling sad and lonely, he tucked himself away, convinced the other butterflies would make fun of him.

Gran Gran Mariposa, a wise and graceful butterfly, was soaring through the meadow when she noticed her grandson's sad little face peeking out from behind the daisy petals.

She flew over and gently landed beside him. "Is my Skylar not having a good day?" she lovingly asked. "What is troubling you, my dear?"

Skylar looked up at Gran Gran Mariposa with tear-filled eyes and replied, "Gran Gran, why are my wings so different? They are not as beautifully decorated as the other butterfly wings."

Her heart filled with love and compassion, Gran Gran Mariposa explained, "My precious Skylar, your wings are different because God designed them, especially for you."

"No two butterfly wings are alike. God paints our wings with Love, and they carry a piece of His heart.

We are then released to the world as a message of God's Love and to shower the Earth with beauty."

Skylar thought about what his Gran Gran said. His eyes gleamed as he looked up at her. "So, my wings are one of a kind? Designed just for me?"

"Yes, my dear," she replied with a loving smile. "Just as snowflake patterns and stars twinkling in the sky are all different, everything God creates is one of a kind.

It's our uniqueness that brings this magical meadow to life.

You can discover the true beauty of your wings by embracing their special uniqueness."

With the words of Gran Gran Mariposa now in his heart, Skylar spread his wings and happily joined the flutter of butterflies in the meadow.

As he glided through the field, Skylar noticed that each butterfly was different in some way.

He was amazed at how the others welcomed him and accepted his differences. They all flew together in harmony, painting a spectacular portrait in the sky.

Skylar felt a newfound love for his wings, and he was no longer afraid to just be himself.

Petal Falls was now even more magical, and Skylar's "misfit" was the perfect fit!"

THE END

About The Author

Debbie R. Magee deeply understands how being a misfit in a seemingly perfect world feels. She struggled with shyness and fear in childhood until she fully embraced her uniqueness. Debbie's journey involved developing a close relationship with Christ, a crucial factor that enabled her to recognize the significant contributions she could make to the world. Today, Debbie inspires young people to love themselves, embrace their individuality, persevere, conquer fear, and dare to dream big. Through her storytelling, she aims to share entertaining yet impactful stories that ignite a spark in children's hearts, motivating them to adopt these qualities and realize their full potential. She is also the author of "YOUNG, GRATEFUL, AND COURAGEOUS" and its sequel, "YOUNG, GRATEFUL, AND COURAGEOUS 2," to which she remains committed, with more exciting books on the horizon. Currently residing in Mississippi, Debbie and her husband are grateful parents to four grown children and grandparents to six adorable grandchildren. They also have a lovable little Maltese named Dewey, each holding a special place in their hearts.

Follow her on Facebook and Instagram @COURAGEOUS BOOKS.
EMAIL: Ladydebbiemagee@gmail.com or info@Ladyenterprises.com

Made in the USA
Columbia, SC
08 April 2024